W9-AVL-993

Ralph Waldo Emerson

The Father of the American Renaissance

The Library of American Thinkers™

Ralph Waldo Emerson

The Father of the American Renaissance

J. Poolos

The Rosen Publishing Group, Inc., New York

Published in 2006 by The Rosen Publishing Group, Inc.
29 East 21st Street, New York, NY 10010

First Edition

Library of Congress Cataloging-in-Publication Data

Poolos, J.
Ralph Waldo Emerson: the father of the American renaissance/by J. Poolos.
    p. cm.–(The Library of American thinkers)
Includes bibliographical references and index.
ISBN 1-4042-0506-3 (lib. binding)
1. Emerson, Ralph Waldo, 1803–1882. 2. Authors, American–19th century–Biography.
3. Transcendentalists (New England)–Biography. I. Title. II. Series.

PS1631.P57 2005
814'.3–dc22

                2005013892

Printed in China

On the cover: A photograph of Ralph Waldo Emerson.

CONTENTS

INTRODUCTION

"Do not go where the path may lead, go instead where there is no path and leave a trail." –Ralph Waldo Emerson

If you were to summarize the accomplishments of Ralph Waldo Emerson in a single thought, you could say that he was the person who put American intellectualism on the map. Born only twenty-eight years after the American Revolution (1775–1783), Emerson became one of the most influential literary figures of the nineteenth century. Although his extensive and wide-ranging readings influenced his ideas, he also drew upon his own life experiences–such as the death of his first wife, and the crisis in faith that led to his resignation from the ministry–to form radical perspectives on theology, philosophy, nature, and the study of literature.

Ralph Waldo Emerson wasn't just a great thinker, he was a figurehead for an entire American philosophical movement. The movement that he helped pioneer, known as transcendentalism, emphasized rational thought, independence, and a love of nature. Emerson produced a number of poems and essays, and frequently gave lectures. His work, along with the work of his fellow transcendentalists, is among the most significant in American literature.

Emerson built a career on the eastern seaboard's lecture circuit, published poetry and essays, and edited a literary magazine. He was also influential in building the first community of intellectuals in America. Based in Concord, Massachusetts, this group included the naturalist-essayist Henry David Thoreau (1817–1862; author of *Walden*), and men and women who would become influential figures in political endeavors, such as the abolition and labor movements.

What separated Emerson from his peers was his refusal to tag along with strictly European ideas. His mission was to forge a philosophy that was distinctly American. He followed on the heels of the great European thinkers of the Enlightenment, who set the stage for new, independent thought. And he used the best of their ideas as a springboard to create his own ideas, which still influence our way of thinking today.

Emerson lived in a time when the United States had just begun to forge its identity. He saw the collective American mind as clay that had yet to be molded, and he took the opportunity to make his mark. Not only did he influence the writers and thinkers of his time, he influenced the generations that followed him in more profound ways than he ever could have imagined. From artists to politicians, a great many notable Americans have taken his views on independence and naturalism, and his philosophy is reflected in their work. His challenge for men and women to be self-reliant is echoed today in such widely diverse arenas as President George W. Bush's proposal for self-managed social security as well as the core message of punk rock music.

Like many great intellectuals of the time, he lived a life of study, wrestling with spiritual and intellectual puzzles, and spreading his ideas through speaking and writing. Ralph Waldo Emerson spent his life doing the difficult work that would inspire generations of leaders in their active roles in social change.

CHAPTER

1

SON OF THE ENLIGHTENMENT

I n order to appreciate the significance of Ralph Waldo Emerson's ideas, it is important to understand the age from which his work was born. Three factors that shaped this age occurred in the seventeenth and eighteenth centuries: the Enlightenment, the Industrial Revolution, and the American Revolution.

The intellectual climate in eighteenth-century Europe went through broad, sweeping changes during the Enlightenment, a movement that brought Europe out of an age of absolute (unquestioning) belief and into an age of reason (thinking). The most important idea of the Enlightenment is that the universe is fundamentally

An eighteenth-century philosopher uses an orrery to lecture a curious audience about the solar system. An orrery is a mechanical teaching aid that can be used to show the location and movement of planets as they revolve around the sun. The scene depicted in this 1766 painting was common during the Enlightenment. People were generally more receptive to scientific ideas than those of previous centuries.

rational. In other words, all things can be understood by means of reason, rather than by faith or tradition. This idea emphasized scientific inquiry and skepticism rather than unquestioning religious dogma. It became the foundation of vast individual, social, political, and economic changes, which included the beginning of a new religious tolerance that would later inspire Emerson.

The second major change that influenced Emerson was the shift from a farming economy to an industrial economy dominated by machines and manufacturing, particularly in England. The Industrial Revolution changed social structure, family structure, consumption habits, and individual habits in a profound way. It was a period of accelerated modernization, with major discoveries in science and philosophy.

The third factor that influenced the world into which Emerson was born was the political revolutions that occurred in

This 1801 painting, entitled *Coalbrookdale by Night*, announced the arrival of the Industrial Revolution. Coalbrookdale is an English town that attracted a lot of attention in the early nineteenth century as a major center of iron production. The fiery glow seen in the background is of a furnace being tapped of its ore. New innovations in iron making would lead to the development of the first railroad around this time.

From Ralph Waldo Emerson's *Nature*

The foregoing generations beheld God face to face; we, through their eyes. Why should not we also enjoy an original relation to the universe? Why should not we have . . . a religion by revelation to us, and not the history of theirs? Embosomed for a season in nature, whose floods of life stream around and through us, and invite us by the powers they supply, to action proportioned to nature, why should we grope among the dry bones of the past?

France and the United States. The European Enlightenment led to the French Revolution (1787–1799), in which the citizens of France overthrew the French monarchy. The Enlightenment also had a significant impact in America. In fact, the United States was built upon Enlightenment ideas of rights, equality, and tolerance.

With the rise of scientific inquiry introduced by the Enlightenment, the advent of the Industrial Revolution, and a new United States without its own intellectual identity, the stage was set for men and women like Emerson to draw upon the best of European thought and forge a new direction for American intellectualism.

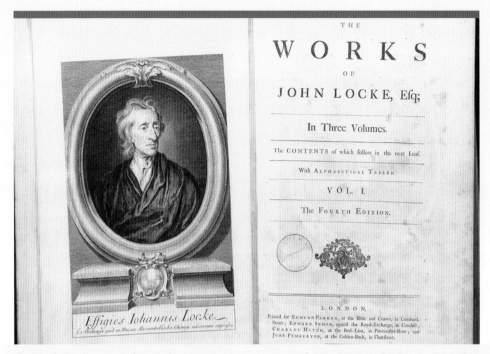

Seen above is an eighteenth-century manuscript of *The Works of John Locke*. John Locke's ideas about government were very controversial during his lifetime. Locke believed that the government had a duty to protect the life, liberty, and property of its citizens. Locke also defended religious freedom and supported the separation of church and state. These themes were eventually incorporated into the U.S. Constitution.

THE PHILOSOPHIES OF JOHN LOCKE AND IMMANUEL KANT

Two philosophers who played a role in shaping Emerson's idealism were John Locke (1632–1704) and Immanuel Kant (1724–1804). The Englishman Locke was one of the most important philosophers of the seventeenth century. Whereas groundbreaking physicist Isaac Newton (1642–1727) described the universe as a machine, Locke went a step further in claiming that the human mind was a machine that essentially gathers information. Locke's far-reaching and influential work *An Essay Concerning Understanding* was considered the first European study of human cognition. Locke promoted the concept of tabula rasa (erased board) in describing the human mind. His essay stated that everyone is born with no preformed ideas and begins life as a blank slate. Furthermore, he believed, all human thought and emotion comes from experience through the five senses.

Plato's Philosophy

The work of the Greek philosopher Plato, his teacher Socrates, and his star pupil Aristotle, formed the basis of all Western philosophy and political thought that has developed over the past 2,000 years. Plato saw a division in the world between material and nonmaterial (spiritual) things. One of Plato's concerns was the ultimate reality of the world and of man's place in it. He professed that the material world is an illusion and that true reality lies in the idea or form of humanness. He called this the "psyche," or soul. Emerson used this perspective to support his ideas that all of nature is not material.

This is an eighteenth-century portrait of the influential philosopher Immanuel Kant. He was an expert in metaphysics and taught it for many years at a Prussian university. Metaphysics is a branch of philosophy that focuses on the structure and nature of reality. Kant believed that the appearances of objects come from a person's perception and not from the object itself.

The Prussian philosopher Immanuel Kant was one of the fathers of the Enlightenment. Kant published an essay called "What Is Enlightenment," which was considered the official mouthpiece of the Enlightenment in Germany. For Kant and other philosophers of the time, the Enlightenment was about knowledge, specifically knowledge about the self. This followed the skeptical philosophy of Locke, but Kant didn't believe wholly in the tabula rasa theory. Kant showed that there existed a class of ideas and forms that came not through experience but through intuition. Emerson went on to pick up where Kant left off.

Emerson used the ancient Greek philosopher Plato's idealist approach in a reaction against Locke's thought. He theorized that although humans do use their senses to experience the world, there is a special connection between humans and the world that cannot be experienced through the senses. In his lectures and writings, Emerson described a process by which humans gain knowledge through personal, divine revelation. The significance of this approach is important. Such thinking transfers religious authority from established religion, and gives it to the individual. Instead of the church defining the overarching relationship between a person and God, the individual makes the rules for his or her own relationship.

Many of Emerson's radical ideas were offensive to the church and to many intellectuals. But with courage and integrity, he blazed his own path where none existed before.

CHAPTER
2

EMERSON'S EDUCATION

Ralph Waldo Emerson was born May 25, 1803, the third of six sons, to William and Ruth Haskins Emerson. The family lived in a house at the corner of Summer and Chauncy streets in Boston, Massachusetts. William Emerson was a prominent Unitarian minister who died in 1811, when young Ralph was eight years old. But it was Ralph's mother, a deeply religious woman, to whom the religious strain in Emerson can be traced.

As a family, the Emersons were a tightly knit clan of readers and thinkers. Though William was a minister, in the presence of his family he remained reserved in his

A painting of the Old State House in Boston shows activity around the historical landmark in 1801. The Boston Massacre took place underneath the building's balcony on March 5, 1770. British soldiers killed five people during a protest of the military occupation. The first public reading of the Declaration of Independence also occurred here on July 18, 1776.

discussions of religion. In his biography, *Emerson: The Mind on Fire*, Robert Richardson writes that Ruth Haskins Emerson was "a strong believer and a practicing, observing Christian" who read books and essays by a wide variety of theologians.

Friends of Emerson's parents, as well as the extended family, were also scholarly and learned in the classics and religious studies. All played a role in young Ralph's upbringing, but none more than his aunt, Mary Moody Emerson. A strong-willed intellectual, she was well read in a wide variety of topics.

A nineteenth-century photograph of Ruth Haskins Emerson. Emerson's mother grew up during the American Revolution and shared those memories with Emerson. She singlehandedly raised him and his five siblings after her husband's death. She also managed to send Emerson and three other sons to Harvard College despite a lack of wealth. She would live with Emerson's family until her death in 1853.

According to Emerson, his aunt could express complex ideas of religious theory and practice as well as any of the heralded theologians whose books he read. Mary was Emerson's only confidante and adviser. He kept a regular correspondence with her, as did his siblings, discussing matters of religion and life choices. She would come to be a shining light in Emerson's moments of darkness and indecision.

With such a strong support system behind him, and with such high expectations of him, it is no wonder young Emerson found success in the classroom. Though he was not the most serious student of the Emerson boys, he did well enough to warrant continued education. When he was fourteen years old,

Emerson entered Harvard College. At the time, Harvard was a boys' school and center of advanced studies with about 250 students. Students typically began their course of study at thirteen or fourteen years of age and graduated at eighteen. Emerson was poor while he was in college. To help pay tuition, he won scholarships and held work-study positions.

During the first two years at Harvard, Emerson's studies included Greek, Latin, physics, philosophy, American constitutional government, religion, and English. He was only a fair scholar and would graduate in the middle of a class of about sixty. But his interests lay outside of his course work. Away from the classroom, he read at least three times the number of books assigned by his professors. These included religious texts such as Joseph Butler's *Analogy*, which argued that Christianity did indeed account for the most recent discoveries in the field of modern science. These books would later influence Emerson's attitudes toward religion. He also began to develop the habit of waking at 4:30 or 5:00 in the morning to write in his journal or write letters to his family.

These signs of disciplined study led to changes in his attitude during his junior year. He became more focused in his thoughts and ambitions. He kept detailed records of impressions of the books he read, and he kept journals of quotations, notes, and original poetry. Emerson was also elected class poet, but only after six classmates had turned down the honor. In fact, during his last year and a half at college, Emerson regarded himself a

This photograph of Emerson was taken at Harvard in the late 1830s, probably at the time Emerson was asked to address the graduating class of Harvard Divinity School. Emerson attended Harvard College as an undergraduate, and later returned to attend the Divinity School, from which he graduated in 1829. Emerson's ideas about religion were very different from what was generally considered acceptable for the time, and the address he delivered to the graduating class of 1838 so scandalized Harvard that four decades passed before he was allowed to make a public appearance there again.

poet more than anything else. And despite the largely practical and rationalist teaching at Harvard, Emerson began to grow more interested in the possibility of the existence of things in nature that we can't really know by our human senses.

In 1819, a young professor named Edward Everett arrived at Harvard to teach Greek literature and religion. Everett was not the traditional, conservative Harvard professor. He was open to various new theories of the origins of Christianity and taught, among other things, the modern theory that the Bible was not one long book written by a single author, but a series of books written by multiple authors over a relatively long period of time. His passion for ancient Greek literature was infectious. Everett's presentation of the Homeric writings—*The Iliad* and *The Odyssey*—moved Emerson. Everett became Emerson's academic inspiration and enabled Emerson to approach his studies with a new openness. As Emerson saw the first glimpses of his independence in the serious matter of thinking, he became more committed to developing his mind. According to Richardson, Emerson vowed in his journal, "I here make a resolution to make myself acquainted with the Greek language and the antiquities and history with long and serious attention to study."

From Harvard Student to Teacher

Emerson finished the last year of college feeling this way, learning through his exploratory readings what he liked and

Here is the Harvard University campus as it appeared in the middle of the nineteenth century. Harvard is the oldest college in the United States. It was founded in 1636 and received its name upon the death of a young minister, John Harvard, who donated his entire library to the school. Of all the colleges and universities in the United States, Harvard has produced the largest number of American presidents among its graduates.

what he wasn't interested in, and attending to his classes and course of study as required. But in August 1821, just three days before his graduation, he heard a speech that would change his life. A master's candidate named Sampson Reed delivered a paper entitled "Oration on Genius," which discussed in broad terms an ideal relationship between man and nature, touching upon ideas of man's individualism and his relationship to God. Reed stated, "The intellectual eye of man is formed to see the light, not to make it." Reed called for a spirituality based on the study of relationships in nature, not on the inventions of man. This union of spirit and nature would later become the foundation of the naturalist view upon which Emerson and writers such as Henry David Thoreau would build their intellectual arguments. At the age of eighteen, Emerson had graduated Harvard College with the

A miniature portrait of William Emerson. William was Emerson's oldest brother and his lifelong friend. They routinely wrote letters to each other until William died. William practiced law in New York and lived in Staten Island. Henry David Thoreau once served as a tutor to William's sons. Thoreau was an influential American philosopher and a close friend of Ralph Waldo Emerson.

seeds of his life's work sown and already showing the first signs of germination.

Immediately following his graduation, Emerson, who had by now asked his family and friends to refer to him as Waldo, returned to Boston to teach at the school for girls that his brother William ran out of their mother's house on Federal Street. He continued his studies, reading vigorously and keeping detailed records of his observations and thoughts in journals.

His readings focused on the philosophers of the school of thought referred to as Scottish Common Sense. These philosophers included Adam Smith, Thomas Brown, and Dugald Stewart. Scottish Common Sense was considered the prevailing school of thought at Harvard, and Emerson was no stranger to its basic principles. Like the German idealism he would later come to admire, this philosophy was based on the great philosopher Francis Bacon's notion that all thought is one of three types: history, philosophy, and poetry. John Locke had taken another approach, breaking thought into the areas of physics, ethics, and logic. Dugald Stewart simplified things by dividing thought into mind and matter. This, too, would greatly influence Emerson's work. It seemed that through his readings, Emerson was charting a direct course toward the fine blend of intellectualism and spirituality that would make him famous. But it wasn't to be so easy.

The closeness of the Emerson family created pressure, not so much based on competition, but based on the expectation that certain high standards would be met. The leader of the family, Aunt Mary, was a motivating force who wanted and expected Waldo and his brothers to commit their lives to the rigorous and noble occupation of the ministry, like their father had. She helped create an environment in which they each kept an eye on the others' progress in career and life choices, either through conversation or correspondence.

William Emerson had begun his studies as a promising scholar of theology, graduating from Harvard and later

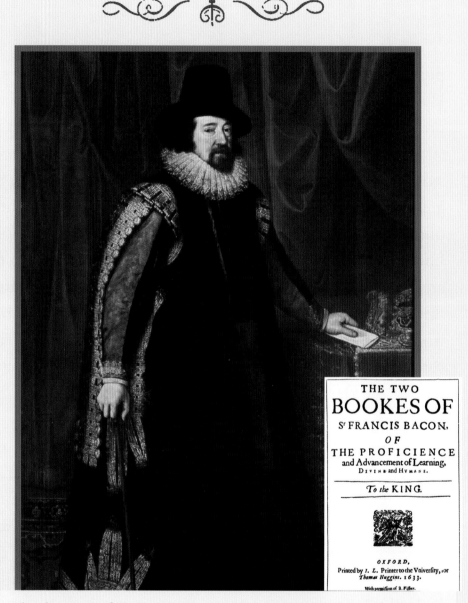

An undated portrait of Sir Francis Bacon and the title page of a 1633 edition of his books *The Proficience* and *Advancement of Learning*. Bacon believed in acquiring knowledge for the benefit of humanity. He developed a way of investigating phenomena called the Baconian method that influenced many future scientists. Bacon died from pneumonia that he contracted while testing the use of snow to preserve meat.

accepting a scholarship to study with the great theologians in Germany. This was a great honor, the sort that was nothing short of daunting for Waldo, who wished to have similar success in his studies. That year in Germany changed William, and he returned to Boston worn down by the lifeless, analytical approach to theology that was unique to the Germans. Consequently, he lost interest in the ministry and took up the practice of law. Being the eldest, William was expected more than anyone else to follow his father into the ministry. So even though William was married and ran a successful law practice, he was considered by family and friends of the family to be something of a failure.

The next-eldest brother was Edward. Of all the Emersons, it was he who had the strongest will to succeed, as well as the talent to back it up. And it was his enormous drive that led to his mental collapse and committal to an asylum. Eventually, he would recover and, like William, take up the practice of law. Still, he was a shattered man, timid and unsure of himself, not at all like the rest of the family. With failing health, he would travel to the warm climate of Puerto Rico to seek a job as a clerk. He died there at age twenty-nine.

Waldo's younger brother Robert was born mentally challenged and required constant care until his death at age fifty-two. The youngest of the family was Charles. He excelled in school, gaining much more acclaim than his brothers. Yet

Emerson was very fond of his brother Edward, and Edward's death came as a great shock. Emerson named his son, Edward Waldo Emerson (seen here in a nineteenth-century daguerreotype), after his beloved brother.

he lacked the work ethic typical of the Emersons. He died of tuberculosis at a young age.

It fell upon young Waldo, then, to carry on with the ministry, and his aunt strongly reminded and encouraged him to steer his career in that direction. For the time being, Waldo was content to continue teaching. It was 1823, and the family had just moved to a house in Roxbury, a long walk from Boston proper. This period marked the beginning of the second major phase of Emerson's training. While he had worked to develop his mind in college, it was now life's circumstances that would force him to make great strides in the development of his spirit.

Unlike his life at Harvard, where he had the friendship of his fellow students and the inspiration of certain faculty to serve as a source of comfort and motivation, Emerson's early adulthood was rife with loneliness. He found it difficult to establish friendships with the other teachers at school. He worked in spiritual and psychological isolation, reading and writing in his journals. He wrote correspondence to old college friends to try to stir up the sort of intellectual conversations they had enjoyed in the past. Unable to find the kind of camaraderie he longed for, Emerson turned inward, picking up a few notebooks he had begun in college. He referred to these notebooks collectively as "Wide World."

The twelve volumes of "Wide World" contained Emerson's thoughts about philosophy and books he had read. Although the notebooks were filled with largely unoriginal thoughts and ideas, Emerson indexed their entirety by topics and reread and later edited them. These notebooks have given Emerson scholars a great insight into the concerns of Emerson and the processes by which he came to conclusions in his early writing. For Emerson himself, they were a learning laboratory. It was here that he began to teach himself how to write the essay, the form of writing he would work in and develop for the rest of his life, a form that he would create and nurture as his own individual contribution to American literature.

CHAPTER
3

THE ROUGH WATERS
OF THE MINISTRY

As Emerson settled into this period of study and self-reflection, he really had no idea what he was looking for. He was still feeling his way along for some idea or system of belief, searching for something as of yet unnamed. As such, he continued to study writings on theology and philosophy with an open mind. He was rewarded with two important revelations that would start him on the path he sought. These complementary discoveries would become the themes of Emerson's life work. One revelation was a new perspective on the relationships of events and things in the world.

The other was a new, brave perception of his own place in the world.

During this time, Emerson made a key finding in his readings that would become the central issue of his study and writings. David Hume (1711–1776), a Scottish philosopher of skepticism, claimed that there is no such thing as a cause-and-effect relationship, and that events are merely sequences of unrelated occurrences. This theory went against the conventional theology of the time, which accepted God as the "first" cause of events, directly or indirectly. Emerson was intrigued by Hume's theories. He wondered how the relationship between people and the world could be determined if there were no cause-and-effect relationships, and no God to set the world in motion. Emerson had no answer, but from that point forward he would spend his life attempting to establish the connection between people and the world.

Emerson's second important revelation of the period was more personal than the first and deserves further examination. It is important to keep in mind that, at the time, Emerson had thrown himself into study and into finding his purpose. While he was sure he needed to prove the existence of the close relationship between man and nature, his fundamental understanding of humankind was deteriorating. Intellectually and spiritually, he was being pulled in several directions. The readings and the lectures he attended presented conflicting views of the order of the world. On the one hand, supporters of the school

This detail from the ceiling of the Sistine Chapel shows God creating the stars and the planets. It took the great artist Michelangelo about five years to paint the ceiling of the chapel, a task he began in 1508. Emerson took a personal approach to religion and did not place much faith in literal interpretations of the Bible.

of thought held by the Unitarian church, including William Channing, were promoting a literal interpretation of the Bible, which offered an account of the life of Jesus Christ. On the other hand, German theologians had introduced a vigorous, new criticism of the Bible and were demonstrating how more and more portions of the book were open to interpretations as "myth, miracle, magic, and folklore" (as quoted in *Emerson: The Mind on Fire*). Emerson was in the midst of a moral crisis.

William Ellery Channing was a Unitarian minister whose liberal views would influence the American transcendentalist movement. Channing was also an author, and he attacked strict church doctrine in his writings and from the pulpit. Although some of Channing's ideas were adopted by the transcendentalists, he himself did not consider himself a transcendentalist.

On top of the intellectual and spiritual dilemmas he confronted, his brother William was about to travel to Germany to study the latest thinking with some of the very theologians and scholars whom Emerson was reading at the time. Meanwhile, Waldo was stuck in Boston, teaching at the girls' school, for which he had little passion. He felt as if he were getting nowhere with his writing. He felt lost in the world and without purpose.

EMERSON'S INNER CONFLICT

Rather than feel remorseful because his brother was off on the kind of adventure he could only dream of living, Emerson challenged himself to succeed with the cards he had been dealt. For the first time, he looked upon his isolation as a gift, an advantage, and a source of strength. As he wrote in his journal in December 1823, "Who is he that shall control me? Why may I not act and speak and write and think with entire freedom? I am solitary in the vast society of beings . . . I am in the midst of them, but not one of them." At last Emerson had found his center.

As his sense of self-reliance grew more concrete with this revelation, Emerson made a commitment to limit his readings to those that focused on the ministry. "I am beginning my professional studies," he wrote in a journal, "and I deliberately dedicate my time, my talent, and my hopes to the Church." In 1824, he gave up his position as a teacher to focus on the study of divinity. And in February 1825, with great hope and promise, Emerson left Roxbury, registered for Harvard Divinity School, and set forth on a career of Unitarian ministry, as his father had before him.

His enthusiasm and clarity of mind were to last only briefly. Within a month of entering the Divinity School, Emerson was struck with uveitis, an inflammation of the eyes that causes severe headaches and loss of vision. The condition was more likely than not brought on by tuberculosis, which was rampant in Boston at the time. Emerson's condition made study impossible. He had two operations to relieve the uveitis, and after a suitable period of rest, he recovered his sight.

Emerson's health improved and he plunged into his studies. During this time, he read Plato (circa 428–348 BC), who, according to Richardson, "was the single most important source of Emerson's lifelong conviction that ideas are real because they are the forms and laws that underlie, precede, and explain appearances." In other words, our ideas of things shape the way we see those things. Therefore, our ideas are as real as the things themselves. Later Emerson would expand upon this notion in his essay "Nature," and in other writings.

In October 1826, Emerson delivered his first sermon. Shortly thereafter, poor health again forced him to temporarily seek a warmer climate, and he sailed to Charleston, South Carolina, to recover. When he returned to Boston, he preached for the first time at the First Church of Boston,

The ancient Greek philosopher Plato was one of the greatest thinkers the world has ever known. One of his major works, *The Republic*, concerns itself with what the best form of government would be. Although modern democracy, as we understand it today, is much different from the kind of democracy practiced in ancient Greece, much of Western culture is based upon the philosophy of Plato and other Greek thinkers.

where his father had been minister. Emerson enjoyed aspects of preaching, particularly the exploration and the communication of ideas. But he found himself on the cusp of a moral dilemma over the relationship between the shepherd and the flock. In his biography *Understanding Emerson*, Kenneth Sacks attributes this dilemma to a lack of self-confidence. Emerson was a man of high morality. He believed, even though he had yet to articulate it in his writings, that individuals should be self-reliant and look for the answers to moral questions within themselves. This conviction left him doubting his true authority as a minister. Still, he continued to preach for the next year in Boston and throughout Massachusetts.

Emerson, a one-time Unitarian minister, had a complex relationship with religious faith throughout his life. Although his family was disappointed that he left the ministry, Emerson would go on to write extensively on religion and spirituality. Boston's King's Chapel, which was at first an Anglican church, became the first Unitarian church in the United States.

At this time, Emerson had begun to write poetry again. While this gave him with great joy and satisfaction, it was also the source of anguish. At this point in his life, he felt the conflict between his life as a minister and his role as poet. On the one hand, there were the institutional trappings of his family, the ministry, and his readings. On the other hand, there were inspiration, original thought, and poetry. Like many poets and artists, he struggled to balance his passion with his responsibilities. This balancing act resulted in confidence and inner growth. While he could not resolve the doubt of his role as a minister and his unstable means of income, he was creating an inner strength that was the result of his surviving the conflict. This strength would enable him to take a big step from the isolation he had lived in for the past few years. He would engage the immediate world, meet new people, and build a social life.

FAITH BORN OF TRAGEDY

On December 25, 1827, Emerson met a woman named Ellen Tucker, who was eight years younger than he was. Tucker and Emerson shared a love for poetry and exchanged many affectionate letters that reflected genuine caring and an eagerness for living. The couple was engaged December 17, 1828. Shortly after, on January 11, 1829, Emerson was hired as junior minister at the Second Church of Boston, a Unitarian church in the city's North End. While Emerson enjoyed the monetary success of the position—his salary was higher than that of the average professor at Harvard—the most profound change he experienced was the sudden shift from a private, secluded, day-to-day life to the bustling life of a public figure. As he was taking in this new lifestyle, Tucker became sick with tuberculosis.

Despite her illness, the two were married in Concord, New Hampshire, on September 30, 1829. They moved into a house on Chardon Street in Boston to begin a new life together. For the next year, Emerson took care of Tucker, also balancing his work in the ministry with his readings. By now his interest in theology had been somewhat pushed to the side by a newfound interest in the natural sciences. He buried himself in books on botany and zoology, and began to write in his journal about the relationship between nature and theology.

On February 8, 1831, after a long illness, and in their seventeenth month of marriage, Ellen Tucker died. Though her death had been expected, the loss affected Emerson profoundly. In his journal, he admitted that he was "unstrung, debilitated by grief" over the death of his wife. Nonetheless, he continued his ministry, not knowing that he was on the verge of confronting a deep, personal religious crisis.

In preparation for a series of lectures on the Gospels, Emerson encountered radically different theories that strongly influenced him. It wasn't long before he came to reject the

Ellen Tucker was still a teenager when she married Ralph Waldo Emerson. Plagued by tuberculosis, she died after the newlyweds had been married for only a short while. Her death was a big blow to Emerson, and although he would remarry, he never quite got over the loss of his young wife.

idea that Christianity was based on the writings of the Bible, and instead believed that Christianity was based on the belief in God. In other words, Emerson believed that a person's faith came from within that person, not from someone else's writings about God. "If we leave the letter and explore the spirit of the apostles and their master," his lecture went, according to Alfred Kazin and Daniel Aaron's book *Emerson: A Modern Anthology*, "we shall find there is an evidence that will come from the heart to the head, an echo to every sentiment taught by Jesus."

It is difficult in this age to comprehend the significance of this point of view. Up to that time, it was widely believed

Emerson's ideas about religion were radical and shocking for the time. Many people interpreted the Bible literally, and believed stories such as Adam and Eve's expulsion from the Garden of Eden, as shown in this nineteenth-century painting. Emerson thought that interpreting the Bible was far less important than an individual's personal relationship with God.

among theologians that the writings of the Bible were the source of Christian faith. In contrast, the new theories that promoted the idea that inner faith was more important than faith in the Bible as an authentic source were nothing short of radical. For a minister like Emerson to discover within himself a belief that contradicted the teachings of the church he served was profound and would most certainly be a reason to doubt one's choice of profession. The act of even considering such theories was a strong statement of independence from the traditional teachings of the church.

EMERSON IN CRISIS

At least one of Emerson's biographers attributes this stroke of independence to the recent events of Emerson's personal life and his resulting emotional state. Richardson notes that "it was Emerson's instinct—and a major key to his strength—that in extreme situations he tended not to reach for traditional supports, not even the Bible, but to reach for his own resources and go it alone." Already Emerson had shown signs of what he would later call self-reliance. His interests began to shift more and more from theology to science, and he discovered a new interest in the natural world around him. He seemed to wake and come alive during his walks in the countryside. He began to read more independently on topics such as astronomy, chemistry, and natural philosophy.

Emerson's personal crises, his readings, and his wife's death all worked together to shake his faith in the views of the church. It wasn't that he couldn't support a religious view of the world. Instead, he renounced the idea that Christianity is centered on the fall of humankind, in Adam and Eve, and in the redemption of humanity through the sacrifice of Christ. How, then, could Emerson continue to lead a church in the face of such personal conflict? For months he agonized, at one point writing in his journal:

It is the best part of the man, I sometimes think, that revolts most against his being the minister. His good revolts from official goodness. We fall into institutions already made and have to accommodate ourselves to them to be useful at all, and this accommodation is, I say, a loss of so much integrity and power.

In June 1832, Emerson gathered his courage and wrote a letter expressing his views to the committee of the Second Church of Boston. On September 9, he delivered a sermon on the subject, which his brother William would call noble. Despite the sermon and Emerson's request for dismissal, the majority of parishioners were reluctant to let him resign, as was the church. But after forty days of deliberations, they granted his request, and Emerson stepped down from the ministry.

With this decision, Emerson had freed himself from the church and the position of leadership over the members of the congregation. He also had stepped out from his father's shadow. In a sense, leaving the church was a great relief, but the entire ordeal, along with his wife's death years before, caused Emerson great anguish. He suffered a severe emotional breakdown that lasted for months.

Sensing he needed a drastic change, Emerson decided on the spur of the moment to give up his house, sell his furniture, and sail abroad. On December 25, 1832, he boarded the *Jasper* and set sail for Malta, Italy, to experience Europe firsthand.

CHAPTER
4

THE ROAD TO TRANSCENDENTALISM

U pon his arrival in Italy, Emerson visited all of the cities in what he called in his journal the "playground of the gods" (as quoted in *Emerson: The Mind on Fire*). He filled his eyes with the paintings, sculptures, statues, unfamiliar landscapes, and the faces of a culture vastly different from the one he knew in Massachusetts. From Italy he journeyed to Switzerland, then to France.

Among the landmarks he visited was the Jardin des Plantes in Paris, a magnificent garden for researchers of botany. There, among the endless species of plant life from various regions of the world living under one roof, he had an epiphany. He realized that his interest in nature, particularly in the interconnectedness of all things, had consumed his attention. Perhaps, for the first time in his life, he embraced this interest. This was a significant moment of self-realization for Emerson, one that would serve him for the remainder of his days. As Richardson describes it, "Over the years, Emerson's openness to science kept his thoughts ballasted [stabilized] with fact and observation and his writing anchored solidly in the real world."

Next, Emerson went to England, where he met the influential poet Samuel Taylor Coleridge (1772–1834). Then he went to Edinburgh, Scotland, where he visited Thomas Carlyle (1795–1881), a radical and influential essayist who wrote with a wild, forceful style. At the time, Carlyle was best known for his 1827 essay "The State of German Literature," in which he advocated that men of literature, not theologians, should be the "interpreters" of divine ideas. He also attacked what he called the current age of materialism and called instead for an age of the mind. These ideas inspired Emerson and fed his desire for social and intellectual reform in America. He described Carlyle in his journal as "an active volcano whose lava torrents of fever frenzy enveloped all things" (as quoted in *Emerson: The Mind on Fire*). The two walked and talked of Plato, America, and various social issues.

The visit with Carlyle lifted Emerson's spirits considerably from those of the downtrodden ex-minister who had sailed from

This nineteenth-century lithograph shows the Jardin des Plantes, a large botanical garden in France. Of special interest to botanists and naturalists, the Jardin des Plantes has existed for hundreds of years. It has thousands of different species of plants from all over the world.

Boston. He wrote in a letter to his brother William that "[I am] in better health than since I was a boy." In fact, he had hit if off so well with Carlyle that Carlyle had written to the social reformist John Stuart Mill (1806–1873), "What I loved in the man was his health, his unity with himself; all people and all things seemed to find their quite peaceable adjustment with him" (as quoted in *Emerson Among the Eccentrics* by Carlos Baker). At last, Emerson had made a lifelong friend who shared his interests and need for radical change.

Immediately following his visit with Carlyle, Emerson traveled to see the great English poet William Wordsworth (1770–1850) at his home in England's Lakes District. The old man treated Emerson with kindness and freely shared his opinions of the great books, the state of public education, and his own work. Emerson was encouraged that the

Emerson met Thomas Carlyle, seen here in an early nineteenth-century photograph, on his trip abroad to Europe. Emerson admired Carlyle, and the two became close friends. However, later in life, Carlyle became bitter and cynical, eventually going as far as writing proslavery essays and attacking democracy. Emerson eventually distanced himself from his one-time friend.

famous poet treated him if not as an equal, then with the respect of a kindred spirit.

Emerson returned to Boston in high spirits. He was excited that he had sought out and engaged the best minds of England. Although he had a great admiration for those with whom he had talked at length, he commented in a letter to his brother Edward, quoted in Richardson's biography, that "not one of them is a mind of the very first class." He concluded that England had not changed his way of thinking but rather had made him more firm in his own convictions. "I feel myself pledged," he wrote, denouncing Unitarianism as an imperfect interpretation of Christianity, "to demonstrate that all necessary truth is its own evidence . . . that Christianity is wrongly received by all such as take it for a system of doctrines . . . it is a rule of life not a rule of faith."

THE LECTURE CIRCUIT

Emerson arrived in Boston on October 9, 1833. His journey had lasted more than nine months, and he was eager to get back to work. Immediately upon his return, he was engaged to give the first lecture of the season at the new Boston Society of Natural History. He approached the task with renewed energy. For the next year he moved from house to house in Boston and Newton. To support himself, he lectured frequently—enough, he thought, to indicate that he may have a career on

Samuel Taylor Coleridge, seen here in an early nineteenth-century oil portrait by Thomas Phillips, was an English poet best known for his work *The Rime of the Ancient Mariner*. A key figure in the English Romantic movement, Coleridge was a contemporary of William Wordsworth. Wordsworth was a proponent of the works of the German philosopher Immanuel Kant, who would be a big influence on Emerson.

the lyceum circuit. His topic was frequently the relationship of the individual and nature. The study of science was more popular than ever, and Emerson included ideas on the values of scientific inquiry and analysis in his lectures whenever he could. He agreed with Thomas Paine (1737–1809), a widely respected intellectual and American founding father, who said that science is the true theology because it studies the work of God. But unlike Paine, Emerson began to see nature as a language, a theme that would repeat itself again and again in his work. In his lectures, he talked about the correspondence between the outer world and the inner world of thoughts and

The English Romantic poet William Wordsworth met Emerson in 1833. It was a great honor for Emerson to meet a poet of Wordsworth's stature, and Emerson was pleased that Wordsworth was willing to discuss literature and other subjects with him. Wordsworth was considered one of the most important British writers of his generation.

The Lyceum

The lyceum grew out of the Enlightenment idea that knowledge should be available to all people, not just the wealthy. Lyceums organized lectures and debates, and some promoted libraries and museums, too. The first lyceum in America was established in Massachusetts in 1826. As the idea spread, lyceums were formed as far west as California. Popular lecturers traveled from the east by railroad to address lyceums all over the country. Lecturers often spoke on topics such as literature, science, and politics.

Emerson was the most frequent speaker at the Concord Lyceum, founded in 1828. For four decades, he spoke twice a year. He also traveled all over the country to lecture at various lyceums. The lyceum was important to Emerson, as it provided him the opportunity to refine his ideas for an audience. Many of the ideas presented in his lectures were the beginnings of his most important publications.

emotions, and about how the writer draws upon nature for language and meaning.

As Emerson began his new life as a lecturer, other aspects of his life came together. His breakout year came in 1834, when he was thirty-one years old. In February of that year, he

A prolific speaker, Emerson gave frequent lectures about his ideas and philosophy. This 1882 illustration shows Emerson giving a speech at the Summer School of Philosophy in Concord, Massachusetts. The school, established by Bronson Alcott, provided a platform for the transcendentalists to spread their ideas.

made a trip to Plymouth, Massachusetts, to preach. There he met Lydia Jackson, with whom he fell in love. It was also the year he came into maturity as a poet. Several of his best poems were written at this time. According to Kenneth Sacks, Emerson explained to Jackson when they were courting, "I am a born poet of a low class without a doubt yet a poet."

At the same time, Emerson came into maturity as a writer of prose. He developed a style of short, declarative sentences first

This 1905 photograph shows Emerson's house in Concord, Massachusetts. The intellectual community in and around Concord proved to be fertile ground for Emerson's literary pursuits.

recorded in his journals—for instance, "We are always getting ready to live but never living." He supported his declarations with concrete images found in the physical world: "What is there of the divine in a load of bricks?" He mastered the imperative mode, which allowed him to communicate his ideas on self-reliance with unarguable conviction: "Insist on yourself. Never imitate," which later appeared in "Self-Reliance."

In late September, the Emersons moved to Concord, Massachusetts. Concord was a small town and the first inland settlement of the Massachusetts Bay Colony. It was also the site of the first battle of the American Revolution. The move made Emerson closer than ever to his brother Charles. The two often read together and exchanged ideas. One week after the move, the family received word from Puerto Rico that Edward had died.

On January 24, 1835, Emerson proposed to Lydia Jackson. The two were well suited. She was an intellectual much like

Although not strictly a transcendentalist, Emerson's second wife, Lydia Jackson, was an extremely intelligent woman in her own right. She helped transform the Emerson household into a place where all of the greatest intellectuals of the area could gather and exchange ideas. The Emersons had frequent guests, most notably Henry David Thoreau, who stayed at the house for long stretches of time.

Emerson. According to a letter written by their friend Margaret Fuller, as quoted by Richardson, the marriage was like "a pilgrimage of two souls toward a common shrine."

THE MATURING INTELLECT

Emerson's reading at the time included the Swedish philosopher Emanuel Swedenborg (1688–1722), who had set out to make a clear connection between the mind and nature and between religion and science. Swedenborg was a great influence on Emerson, who by this time was becoming a philosophical idealist, strong in his convictions of a better understanding of the world.

On September 14, 1835, he and Lydia (or, as he called her, Lydian) were married. The newlyweds moved into a house in Concord, where they entertained frequent visitors. Emerson re-indexed his journals, worked on his book *Nature*, and wrote a lecture on English literature. This was significant because at the time there was no such study in academia. He viewed English writers such as Geoffrey Chaucer and William Shakespeare, as well as the modern writers, as the fathers of an American literature that had not yet been born. His lecture "The American Scholar" emphasized the power of ideas for writers: "It is the writer, the poet, who converts the solid globe, the land, the sea, the sun, the animals, into symbols of thought" (as quoted in *Emerson: The Mind on Fire*).

Emanuel Swedenborg was a tremendous influence on Emerson, who had been questioning the nature of his relationship to God. Swedenborg was a Swedish scientist and philosopher. He abandoned his scientific work, however, after undergoing what he considered to be religious and mystical experiences.

During the winter of 1835 to 1836, Emerson continued a regular correspondence with Thomas Carlyle, and he worked to generate interest in an American edition of Carlyle's powerful work *Sartor Resartus* (The Tailor Retailored). He wrote the introduction to the edition and had the privilege of sending the first printed copy to Carlyle.

In May 1836, Charles Emerson died suddenly of an illness. The death of his brother was devastating to Emerson. To keep his mind off the pain, he plunged into *Nature*, which had become an exploration of the relationship of nature to human beings. The book is an "inquiry into the laws of the world and the frame of things," he wrote, according to Richardson.

Emerson established that both science and religion exist only to describe and explain nature, which he called wild and beautiful, much like man's inner self. He directed the intellects of his generation not to dwell on past generations' interpretations of the world and God, but to create their own original relationship to the universe. In essence, he bravely called for an original American philosophy and literature, not a copy. True to the ideas Emerson promoted, the book itself is not a response to another book, but a collection of wholly original ideas, a subject he created from scratch.

THE MEANING OF NATURE

The significance of Emerson's view of nature as a commodity cannot be understated. First, at the time it was widely accepted that nature was an eternally renewable resource. No one had considered that humans could alter nature in meaningful ways, let alone damage it. Emerson may have been the first person to write about nature as a collection of raw materials at the disposal of humans. This implied a responsibility of all humankind to protect natural resources and to became part of the foundation of the environmental movement, built upon later by Henry David Thoreau and Walt Whitman (1819–1892), among others.

Second, Emerson treated nature as a philosophical phenomenon. In *Nature*, he described it as an entity that furnishes us with standards of beauty, physical limits, and morality. "The world thus exists to the soul to satisfy the desire of beauty," he wrote, implying that we use objects found in nature as guidelines for the measurement of our own inner beauty. He went on to claim that we use nature to describe our feelings, ideals, and thoughts because "nature itself is a language, an expression of the laws or forms or ideas that lie beneath the visible world." He identifies nature not as a collection of things—trees, oceans, and stars, for instance—but as a process that results in creation, change, and death.

Historically, *Nature* can be read as a modern take on Stoicism. This fourth-century school of thought was built on the premise that all ideas and things could be divided into two categories: those that can be changed and those that cannot be changed. Stoicism focuses on things that can be changed, emphasizing ethics and a code of how to live rather than epistemology (the study of knowledge). Stoicism also endorses the individual will and self-rule among humans. But in *Nature*, Emerson had refined these basic ideas and made them his own.

THE BIRTH OF THE TRANSCENDENTAL GROUP

With *Nature*, Emerson had written his first major work, but already he was looking for alternative ways to share his ideas. On September 8, 1836, the day before *Nature* was published, he met with Concord intellectuals Henry Hedge, George

Putnam, and George Ripley in Cambridge to plan a periodic gathering of people who, like them, were dissatisfied with the conservative environment at Harvard.

Eleven days later they met again at Ripley's house. Ten people, including Bronson Alcott, Orestes Brownson, and a few Divinity School students, held an informal, open forum for the exchange of their ideas. Most in the group were ministers or intellectuals. In *Emerson: The Mind on Fire*, Richardson notes that the "member list reads like a who's who list of intellectuals of the time." They came together because they were dissatisfied with the state of philosophy, religion, and literature in America. They recognized that American intellectuals had always looked to Europe for direction, and their aim was to forge an American intellect that was original and distinct from foreign influence.

The ideas of these people were considered radical. In fact, the group's members would prove to be politically radical as well. Many of them would later become key members in the

George Ripley, seen here in an engraving from 1880, is best known for creating a community called Brook Farm. Like Emerson, Ripley had been a Unitarian minister. He had intended Brook Farm to be a secluded, intellectual community, relying on agriculture. Unfortunately, the intellectuals of Brook Farm discovered that they were ill-suited to difficult, menial labor, and the community eventually fell apart.

An Excerpt from Emerson's 1842 Lecture "The Transcendentalist"

The Transcendentalist adopts the whole connection of spiritual doctrine. He believes in miracle, in the perpetual openness of the human mind to new influx of light and power; he believes in inspiration, and in ecstasy. He wishes that the spiritual principle should be suffered to demonstrate itself to the end, in all possible applications to the state of man, without the admission of anything unspiritual; that is, anything positive, dogmatic, personal. Thus, the spiritual measure of inspiration is the depth of the thought, and never, who said it? And so he resists all attempts to palm other rules and measures on the spirit than its own . . .

It is well known to most of my audience, that the Idealism of the present day acquired the name of Transcendental, from the use of that term by Immanuel Kant, of Konigsberg, who replied to the skeptical philosophy of Locke, which insisted that there was nothing in the intellect which was not previously in the experience of the senses, by showing that there was a very important class of ideas, or imperative forms, which did not come by experience, but through which experience was acquired; that these were intuitions of the mind itself; and he denominated them Transcendental forms. The extraordinary profoundness and precision of that man's thinking have given vogue to his nomenclature, in Europe and America, to that extent, that whatever belongs to the class of intuitive thought, is popularly called at the present day Transcendental . . .

women's movement, the antislavery movement, the labor rights movement, and the movement for Native American rights. The meetings centered on a single topic such as the education of humanity or the nature of poetry. Emerson attended twenty or so meetings over the next four years.

The group would become informally known as the Transcendental Group. Transcendentalism was a philosophy based on the belief in a higher reality than can be found through a human's senses or experiences. The transcendentalists took the view that something existed beyond the senses that an individual could know intuitively. Thus, a greater power exists to unify individual souls. This "oversoul" exists in everything. We can look to the ancient Greek philosopher Plato and his concept of idealism for an example of a thing that is "transcendental." Plato said that God is transcendental—God exists outside of nature. This same idea is a fundamental principle in orthodox forms of the world's major religions: Christianity, Judaism, and Islam. The philosopher Immanuel Kant had founded the theory as a reaction to John Locke's

Boston was home to many influential American writers and intellectuals during the nineteenth century. This 1875 engraving shows some of the city's brightest minds, including the author Oliver Wendell Holmes *(left, standing)*, Ralph Waldo Emerson *(second from left, seated)*, Nathaniel Hawthorne *(second from right, seated)*, and Henry Wadsworth Longfellow *(right, seated)*.

pronouncement that, following Newton, man's mind was like a machine and that everything he knows he knows through his experience.

American transcendentalism was also influenced by aspects of Romanticism. The artistic, social, and political movement known as Romanticism began in Germany and England in the 1770s, and had swept the Western Hemisphere by the 1820s. It celebrated self-examination, individualism, and the beauty of both nature and humankind. Its supporters saw a direct correspondence between the universe and the soul. Intuition rather than reason was looked upon as the highest human quality. Emerson himself wrote in a journal early in his career that man must use nature to see what is beyond nature.

The Transcendental Group would become a sounding board for Emerson as he worked out his ideas over the next several years.

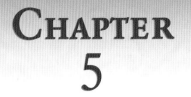

CHAPTER 5

EMERSON: SAGE OF CONCORD

In 1836, Emerson was thriving. Despite the mixed reviews *Nature* had garnered—it was called selfish and illogical, among other things—the overall reception was enthusiastic. Emerson found the Transcendental Group's conversations stimulating. His spirits were further bolstered by the birth of his first child, whom he named Waldo. At this time, his writing was fiery and direct. As he had with *Nature*, he continued to forge his own path. His main area of focus was a series of twelve lectures on the philosophy of history. The lectures elaborated on the theme that the way we look at history limits our understanding of the past. He said

NATURE.

"Nature is but an image or imitation of wisdom, the last thing
of the soul; nature being a thing which doth only do, but not
know."

PLOTINUS.

BOSTON:
JAMES MUNROE AND COMPANY.

M DCCC XXXVI.

Nature became known as one of Emerson's most important works, although it did not always receive favorable reviews upon its publication. Some of the writing in *Nature* is dense and complicated, and many of the ideas it contains were ahead of its time. However, *Nature* is credited as a landmark of American literature, and is viewed as one of the definitive works produced by the transcendentalists.

that history looks too much at "the man or woman on the throne," referring to kings and queens, and not at human nature. History, he said, should be the record of the "one mind" we all share (as quoted in *Emerson: The Mind on Fire*).

At this time, he became close friends with Henry David Thoreau, whom he had known about a year. Thoreau was an exceptionally bright twenty-year-old senior at Harvard. The two men shared similar interests. They spent many hours walking in the woods, identifying plants, and discussing philosophy. These conversations would later influence both men's writing.

DECLARATIONS OF INDEPENDENCE

In 1837, Emerson was invited to deliver an address on the American scholar to the Phi Beta Kappa Society. This address was part of the commencement ceremonies for the Harvard class that included Thoreau. Titled simply, "The American Scholar," the speech was one of Emerson's most successful and influential contributions to literature. Emerson's statement was so clear, powerful, and convincing that Harvard professor Oliver Wendell Holmes called it "our intellectual declaration of independence." In his lecture, Emerson stated that "our day of dependence, our long apprenticeship to the learning of other lands, draws to a close" and that "we have listened too long to the courtly muses of Europe" (as quoted in *Emerson: The Mind on Fire*).

Next, Emerson challenged the current views of Christianity. On July 15, 1838, he was invited to address the graduating seniors at Harvard Divinity School. He took the opportunity to attack formal Christian beliefs, asserting that the absolute authority of the Bible and the concept of the divinity of Jesus get in the way of true religious feeling. He claimed that the New Testament, though a great work, offered only a secondhand God. In other words, followers of Christianity experienced the religion, not God. Emerson further emphasized that individuals should not look to a single book as the ultimate source of truth. Instead, they should examine the process of creating the book.

This lecture was a radical departure from conventional lines of thought. Emerson wasn't preaching atheism that day, but instead a personal connection with religion, celebrating life and his belief that people are always surrounded by divinity. He promoted a universal feeling of religion that he believed exists with every human.

At the same time, his lecture criticized the foundation of Christianity, although he recognized that Jesus Christ's life illustrated his central teaching, that the divine (God) exists in the human (Jesus). Emerson believed that when theologians depict Jesus as separate from the rest of humanity, mythologize the man, and treat him as a god, Christ's message is lost. He recommended to his audience that each individual should find his or her own interpretation of God and religion: "Let me admonish you to go alone, to refuse the good models, even those which are sacred to the imagination of men, and dare to love God without mediator or veil." He insisted that "Christianity was founded on human nature, not on the Bible." "They call it Christianity," he said. "I call it consciousness" (as quoted in *Emerson: The Mind on Fire*).

The uproar this address caused was like nothing Emerson had seen before. Fearing the worst criticism, he retired to Concord, where he worried that the address would alienate his audience. His friends and admirers offered their support, and soon the whole thing blew over.

"SELF-RELIANCE"

In addition to his lectures, Emerson was busy with other projects. On February 24, 1839, Lydian gave birth to their second child, whom they named Ellen, after Ellen Tucker, Emerson's first wife. In the journals and letters Emerson wrote during this time, life at home is described as peaceful and serene. He would read and write in his first-floor study, sitting at his writing table in a rocking chair in the center of the room. Books covered one entire wall; on the others, pictures hung. He continued to organize the publication of translations of Carlyle's writings. He began to realize that with the exception of *Nature* and his poems, all of his ideas had been presented as lectures.

It was time, he decided, to write essays. He set to work indexing his old journals by topic. This was a task Emerson

Quotes from "Self-Reliance"

"That which we persist in doing becomes easier for us to do; not that the nature of the thing itself is changed, but that our power to do is increased."

"Nothing at last is sacred but the integrity of your own mind."

"A foolish consistency is the hobgoblin of little minds, adored by little statesmen and philosophers and divines. With consistency a great soul has simply nothing to do."

would revisit for the rest of his writing life. By 1847, he would have a 400-page master index of topics contained in about 265 journals. By July 1847, he had written three essays: "History," "Self-Reliance," and "Compensation." Of the three, "Self-Reliance" is the best known. In it, Emerson advocates reliance on the individual self—but not selfish or anticommunity behavior—as a starting point for everybody. "Nothing is sacred but the integrity of your own mind," he wrote. He went on to say that a better society will be the result not of a suppression of individualism but of a voluntary coming together of fulfilled individuals. He followed with more essays, including "Love" and "Friendship."

During this productive period, Emerson became involved with the founding of a magazine. He had long wanted to start a magazine to publish progressive ideas. On May 4, 1840, the *Dial* was created. The goal was to publish the ideas held by the Transcendental Group. On July 1, the first issue appeared. The content was forward-looking and reform-minded. It was edited by Margaret Fuller, and included a poem and essay by Thoreau, an essay by Bronson Alcott, verse by Ellen Tucker, and some of Charles Emerson's writing. Emerson composed the editorial statement himself.

In 1841, *Essays* was published to great acclaim, and later that year the couple's third child, Emily, was born. But 1842 brought tragedy when young Waldo came down with scarlet fever and died. "You can never know how much of me a young child can take away," Emerson wrote to Thomas Carlyle (as quoted in *Emerson: The Mind on Fire*). In February, Emerson collected himself and journeyed to New York to deliver a series of lectures. Upon his return, Margaret Fuller announced she was stepping down as editor of the *Dial*. Rather than let the magazine die, Emerson took her place.

At the time, the magazine had about 300 subscribers and brought in just enough money to cover the cost of printing and binding. Over the next two years, Emerson would spend about half of his working hours on the magazine. He contributed some fifty pieces, and also solicited new material. His *Dial* was different from Fuller's. For instance, it included

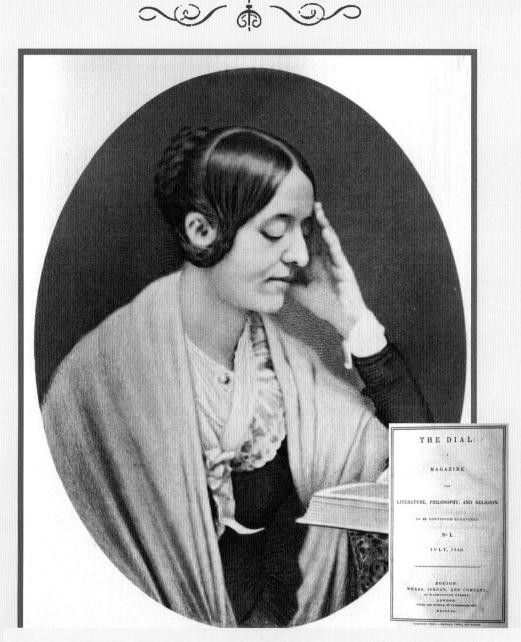

THE DIAL:

MAGAZINE

FOR

LITERATURE, PHILOSOPHY, AND RELIGION.

TO BE CONTINUED QUARTERLY

Nº I.

JULY, 1840.

BOSTON:
WEEKS, JORDAN, AND COMPANY,
141 WASHINGTON STREET.
LONDON:
WILEY AND PUTNAM, 67 PATERNOSTER ROW.
M DCCC XL.

Margaret Fuller was a journalist, women's rights activist, and instrumental figure in the Transcendental Group. The editor of the *Dial* for two years, Fuller is perhaps best known for her book *Woman in the Nineteenth Century*, a powerful argument for women's rights. The first issue of the *Dial (inset)*, published in 1840, contained work by Fuller, Emerson, Thoreau, and others.

Margaret Fuller:
Transcendentalist and Intellectual

Author, critic, and political activist, Margaret Fuller was a forceful influence on the liberal-minded transcendentalists and the Concord community as a whole. Born in 1810, she received the kind of intense and comprehensive education that at the time was almost exclusive to young men. She and Emerson were introduced by a common acquaintance and grew to be great friends. When the Transcendental Group founded the *Dial* in 1840, Fuller was named editor, a position she held for two years.

She was a literary critic at the *New York Tribune*, one of the most influential publications in the country, run by American founding father of journalism, Horace Greeley. In 1845, she published *Woman in the Nineteenth Century*, an important book central to the women's rights movement. Later, she accepted a position with Greeley as a foreign correspondent in Europe. While in England, she met and fell in love with an Italian revolutionary, and she became a revolutionary activist. The couple had a son. She wrote home that she had married, but some historians speculate that she only said she was married to make her return home easier.

When the republic they supported collapsed, they fled to the United States. Tragically, their ship was wrecked on a sandbar in New York Harbor only a few hundred feet offshore, and her body was never recovered. Fuller's legacy lives on in intellectualism, feminism, and political activism.

excerpts of scripture from the world's major religions. One issue featured excerpts from the Hindu Vishnu Sarma; another, from the Hindu Laws of Menu; another, from the Persian Desatir; and still another contained selections from the writings of Confucius. The magazine was a clearinghouse for new ideas. There were scientific news items, such as a report of a recent expedition to Antarctica; there were book reviews; and there was less writing on art and music, and more literature.

A Tribute to Great Men

By the mid-1840s, Emerson's commitment to individualism was facing growing skepticism by his younger colleagues, such as Bronson Alcott and W. H. Channing, the son of his old friend William. At the same time, his views of individualism were becoming less innocent. His focus had shifted from the collective mind to individual freedoms and differences between individuals.

On August 1, 1844, Emerson delivered a heated address calling for the abolition of slavery. He had always strongly objected to the concept and practice of slavery, but for the first time in his life he was taking an active role in the movement to ban slavery.

Many factors may have influenced Emerson's decision to become an active participant in what he thought was a perfectly good fight. After all, it was the great thinkers of the Enlightenment who professed the importance of equality between people. But Emerson's more recent readings may have played a larger role in his decision. Two such influential books were *History of the Abolition of the African Slave Trade*, by Thomas Clarkson, and *Emancipation in the British West Indies*, by James Thome and J. H. Kimball. Perhaps more important was Emerson's recent introduction to the writings of Lucretia Mott (1793–1880), a powerful abolitionist and women's rights advocate whose opinions Emerson greatly respected.

Emerson was asked to deliver the address on the tenth anniversary of the British emancipation of slaves in the West Indies. The talk was sponsored by the Women's Anti-slavery Association. His rousing speech was intended to call citizens to action. It was well received by supporters of abolition who petitioned Emerson to continue supporting abolition by public means. Emerson never devoted a major work to the subject of abolition, but he supported the movement through letters and through his influence as a speaker.

On October 19, 1844, *Essays: Second Series* was published. Emerson continued to write and lecture. As a change of pace,

Lucretia Mott, seen here in a photograph from around 1860, influenced Emerson to become a supporter of the abolitionist movement. Mott's book *Discourse on Women*, which examined the unequal status of women in society, was published in 1850, bringing Mott a measure of celebrity. A tireless activist, Mott worked for social justice until her death in 1880.

he planned to publish a volume of original poetry. But his primary occupation was the writing of a lecture on influential, great men. His old friend Thomas Carlyle had urged him to write a biography of a single American hero with the aim of elevating that man into worldwide fame and drawing the attention of European intellectuals. Instead, Emerson's lectures included no Americans. He was more impressed by Plato, Swedenborg, Shakespeare, Napoléon, and the German writer and philosopher Johann Wolfgang von Goethe, among others.

The goal of these lectures was to reconcile the differences between the accomplishments of these great men and those of the common man in democratic societies, where all men were considered equal. Emerson called the series of lectures Representative Men. His main point was that great people are not superior to common people; they are representative of the best traits in many common people.

The Representative Men lectures were not Emerson's only talks of 1845. His lecture schedule became more demanding as the years passed. By the 1850s, he was delivering some eighty

Labor conditions in British factories were usually terrible during the Industrial Revolution. The manufacturing boom created a number of jobs in cities such as London. Factories, such as the Thames Iron Works seen in this 1866 photo, were common fixtures in any urban area. Cities soon became overcrowded and polluted, and workers were exploited by greedy factory owners. Emerson witnessed these conditions firsthand on his second trip to London.

lectures a year. He lectured all over Massachusetts and New York. Eventually he would travel west to Iowa, Missouri, and even to California. No matter what part of the country he was in, his lectures almost always drew strong reactions. Some reviews glowed with praise; others were highly critical of his unorthodox points of view.

In 1846, *Poems* was published. In contrast to his essays and lectures, Emerson's poems gave voice to his ecstatic side. They were daring and at times even wild. Following their publication, Emerson found himself restless and, as always, looking for a new challenge. He thought another journey to Europe would stimulate his mind. On October 5, 1847, he left for Liverpool, England, on the *Washington Irving* to deliver lectures abroad.

A Return to England

By this time, the Industrial Revolution in England was in full swing. It was the England of Charles Dickens, and it seemed overcrowded, busy, and impoverished to the nature-loving Emerson. He stayed for a time in Liverpool, lecturing in nearby Manchester. To his surprise, the *Dial* was very well known there, and he was treated as a hero of sorts. On the positive side, there were dinners in his honor. On the negative side, his radical ideas were frequently attacked by ministers in their sermons. He would deliver sixty-seven lectures in

England and Scotland. Along the way, he met many of the great minds of the time: the poet Lord Alfred Tennyson (1809–1892), novelist William Makepeace Thackeray (1811–1868), and poet Matthew Arnold (1822–1888) to name a few. He left quite an impression. While Emerson stood on the deck of the ship that would bring him home, Richardson reports in his biography, Emerson conversed with Arthur Hugh Clough (1819–1861), a poet and someone Emerson considered a new friend. Clough told him, "You leave all us young Englishmen without a leader."

If there was a drawback to the trip for Emerson, it was his meetings with his old friend Thomas Carlyle, who had become overwhelmingly pessimistic and burdened in the fifteen years since the two had met. Now they had little in common. They parted, civil to one another, but no longer friends.

After nearly a year abroad, Emerson returned to Concord to find his friendships newly recharged. The exception was Thoreau. Nearly three years prior, Thoreau had built a cabin

Emerson was a friend and mentor to Henry David Thoreau, seen here in a photograph from 1856. Thoreau was a gifted writer who would go on to be America's first naturalist. Emerson was responsible for giving Thoreau his start in the literary world and championed Thoreau's work, which did not meet with popular or critical success. Despite their occasional quarrels, the two men remained close throughout their lives, and Emerson delivered the eulogy at Thoreau's funeral.

on Walden Pond and lived there for more than two years. Then Emerson asked Thoreau to move into his own home to watch over Lydian and the children while Emerson was in England. Now that Emerson had returned, it appeared to him that Thoreau was resentful. It seemed Thoreau spited Emerson's worldliness and travels to Europe, while Emerson had no tolerance for Thoreau's withdrawing from society to live, isolated, in his cabin.

In 1851, Emerson began work on "The Conduct of Life," a lecture that dealt with more practical issues than was typical of him, such as productivity, social riches, and economics. Emerson was no doubt influenced by the shift from sustenance farming to industrial farming in America. With this change, families no longer farmed a variety of crops solely to feed themselves, but instead grew crops and sold the produce to earn money to buy other goods and services. Now there were new definitions of emotional and spiritual success to explore.

In his biography of Emerson, Kenneth Sacks states that "Emerson's contributions to emancipation are often over-looked." That year, Emerson became more active in the support of abolition. Many of the Emersons' transcendentalist friends, among others, were main participants of the Underground Railroad, an escape system for fugitive slaves. Concord was on one of the five routes out of Boston.

After Thomas Sims, a fugitive slave who had come to Boston as a stowaway, was arrested and publicly whipped, the

Walden and "Civil Disobedience": Thoreau's Legacy

Henry David Thoreau (1817–1862) was an American writer and philosopher best known for two works: *Walden* and "Civil Disobedience." *Walden; or, Life in the Woods* was published in 1854. It is a collection of autobiographical writings that describe in great detail his observations during the two-year period when he lived in a small cabin on Walden Pond in Concord, Massachusetts. This exercise in isolationism and a studied observance of nature, along with some of his other works on nature, made Thoreau the first naturalist.

"Civil Disobedience" was a Concord Lyceum lecture delivered by Thoreau on January 26, 1848. It was published as "Resistance to Civil Government" in May 1849. This impassioned plea for a better government through less but more thoughtful governing has influenced some of the world's great minds, including former Indian leader Mohandas Gandhi and civil rights activist Martin Luther King Jr. It was King who said in his autobiography, "No other person has been more eloquent and passionate in getting this idea across than Henry David Thoreau. As a result of his writings and personal witness, we are the heirs of a legacy of creative protest."

The Underground Railroad was a system of secret routes and safe houses used to help escaping slaves reach freedom. Most routes led to Northern free states or Canada, although some also led to Mexico. More than 100,000 slaves made their way to freedom through the Underground Railroad.

citizens of Concord petitioned Emerson to speak publicly on his ideas of abolition. On May 3, he delivered a talk in Concord that called on the State of Massachusetts to honor its revolutionary past by repealing the Fugitive Slave Act of 1850. This act provided that any slave who escaped to another state or federal territory would be returned to his or her owner. Richardson's biography summarizes what may be Emerson's underlying motivation for speaking out for the freedom of all people: "Emerson's long campaign against slavery is a practical and concrete result of his even longer habit of affirming freedom of will and action in opposition to determinism."

EMERSON AND WALT WHITMAN

By the mid-1850s, Emerson had become famous. Reviews of his lectures at home and abroad were widespread. He was gaining a strong reputation in France, where, according to Richardson, one poet called him "the most original man produced by the United States to this day." By 1854, Emerson had received 644 review notices from magazines and journals. Herman Melville, renowned author of *Moby Dick*, satirized Emerson in his work *The Confidence Man*. Considering Emerson's fame and reputation as a thorough and radical thinker, it was no surprise that writers solicited his opinions of their own work.

One such writer was the young poet Walt Whitman. On July 4, 1855, a thin, anonymous volume of poems was delivered to Emerson's home in Concord. It was Whitman's revolutionary work *Leaves of Grass*. Emerson was so impressed with the poetry that he sent it to friends for their opinions. He wrote Whitman, praising the poet for his extraordinary contribution to American letters. Whitman was overjoyed at the response, and he used the letter to promote his reputation. He had the *New York Tribune* print the letter. He also had the letter printed up as a flyer. Finally, he had the second edition of *Leaves of*

Grass printed with a quotation from the letter and with Emerson's name printed on the spine of the book. Though Emerson once commented that Whitman's exploitation of his name and reputation was a bit rude, his enthusiasm for the work was not diminished.

Emerson and Whitman would go on to become friends. Richardson states that "Emerson is a constant, almost obsessive presence" in Whitman's journals and correspondence. Though Whitman would play down Emerson's influence on him, according to Richardson, he once said, "I always go back to Emerson. He was the one man to do a particular job on his own account." Whitman would become the voice of his generation and, to this day, the most lauded American poet.

LATER YEARS

During his later years, Emerson developed a sense of urgency. He lectured more frequently than ever, traveling to California

Walt Whitman, seen here in an 1849 photograph, was a great admirer of Emerson. Whitman did not receive much schooling, but read widely. An intensely lyrical poet, Whitman is one of the most significant voices in American literature. Whitman was a great believer in democracy and personal freedoms, and he served as a nurse in the Union army during the Civil War.

O the bleeding drops of red!

O CAPTAIN! MY CAPTAIN!

BY WALT WHITMAN.

I.

O CAPTAIN! my captain! our fearful trip is done,
The ship has weathered every track, the prize we sought is won,
The port is near, the bells I hear, the people all exulting,
While follow eyes the steady keel, the vessel grim and daring.
    But O heart! heart! heart!
    Leave you not the little spot,
    Where on the deck my captain lies,
    Fallen cold and dead.

II.

O captain! my captain! rise up and hear the bells;
Rise up! for you the flag is flung, for you the bugle trills:
For you bouquets and ribboned wreaths, for you the shores a-crowding:
For you they call, the swaying mass, their eager faces turning.
    O captain! dear father!   *beneath your head*
    This arm I push beneath you,
    It is some dream that on the deck
    You've fallen cold and dead.

III.

My captain does not answer, his lips are pale and still:
My father does not feel my arm, he has no pulse nor will.
But the ship The ship is anchored safe, its voyage closed and done: *and*
From fearful trip the victor ship comes in with object won! *sound.*
    Exult, O shores! and ring, O bells!
    But I, with silent tread,
    Walk the spot my captain lies
    Fallen cold and dead.

This photograph of a Walt Whitman manuscript shows an early version of Whitman's poem "O Captain! My Captain!", which describes his reaction to the assassination of President Abraham Lincoln. Whitman is best known for his book *Leaves of Grass*, which he published with his own money. The book did not sell many copies until it was published along with Emerson's praise.

and later to Egypt. In 1867 alone, he delivered eighty lectures. He also released a second volume of poems, *May-Day and Other Pieces*. This book included two long poems as well as some of Emerson's best-known short poems, such as "Brahma," "Days," and "Terminus." But this book would signal the end of his truly productive days.

Over the next few years, Emerson's energy and powers declined. He experienced embarrassing memory losses. By 1874, he avoided social situations, preferring instead to stay at home. He lectured only on special occasions, often lacking the power to be heard beyond the first few rows. Yet he was happy and content to be at home with his children and grandchildren.

In mid-April 1882, while on a walk, Emerson was caught in a rainstorm. He came down with pneumonia, and on April 27, he died.

EMERSON'S LEGACY

Ralph Waldo Emerson left a legacy unparalleled in American letters. His influence on the thinkers and writers not only of his generation, but of the generations to follow, cannot be overestimated. He essentially changed the landscape of American intellectualism, theology, ecology, and rhetoric. His brand of idealism was extremely influential during the middle of the nineteenth century. American authors and poets such as Melville, Nathaniel Hawthorne, Emily Dickinson, and of course Thoreau and Whitman, were indebted to his work. The core of his philosophy was important to Europeans as well, including the philosopher Friedrich Nietzsche, and the writers Marcel Proust and Virginia Woolf.

Emerson's influences are inescapable and extend from politics to the arts. One shining example can be seen in the work of the well-known architect Frank Lloyd Wright, whose Unity Temple in Oak Park, Illinois, is the direct expression of some of Emerson's most important ideas. Because the structure functions as a Unitarian church (the very church on which Emerson turned his back), it is a special example of Emerson's influence.

The Unity Temple, built in 1908 in Oak Park, Illinois, was designed by the famed architect Frank Lloyd Wright. The inside of the church is not large, but includes a number of balconies. Wright intentionally designed the structure this way so that everyone in the church would be close to the pulpit. A marvel of modern architecture, Unity Temple serves as a Unitarian church.

Consider the interior of this Unitarian church. Aisles run along the walls from front to back. The floor where the pews stand is elevated, representing the higher spiritual plane of the individual communing with God. Where most churches have steeples reaching to the sky in a gesture of a worshipper reaching upward to God, Wright's temple has a giant skylight, a window between the individual and God. These are just two features that demonstrate Wright's adaptation of Emerson's

concepts of humankind's communion with nature and the divine. Spirituality was not the product of a systematic study of theology but instead of an intuitive harmony between humankind, nature, and God.

Emerson's legacy supports his own view of the world as a continuum in the constant state of creation. As he wrote in an essay called "The Poet," "For the world is not painted or adorned, but is from the beginning beautiful; and God has not made some beautiful things, but Beauty is the creator of the universe."

TIMELINE

1803 Ralph Waldo is born in Boston, Massachusetts, to William and Ruth Haskins Emerson.

1817–1821 Emerson attends Harvard College.

1822–1825 Emerson teaches school.

1825 Emerson admitted to Harvard Divinity School to pursue theological studies.

1826 Emerson preaches his first sermon.

1829 Emerson marries Ellen Tucker.

1831 Ellen Tucker dies.

1832 Emerson resigns from the Second Church of Boston; begins his trip to Italy, France, England, and Scotland; and starts a career of lecturing.

1835 Emerson marries Lydia Jackson.

1836 Emerson publishes *Nature* and helps form the Transcendental Group. Emerson's first son, Waldo, is born.

1837 Emerson delivers "The American Scholar" lecture at Harvard. Henry David Thoreau is in the audience.

1838 Emerson delivers the Divinity School address at Harvard.

1840 Emerson helps found the *Dial*.

1841 Emerson publishes *Essays*.

1842 Emerson's son Waldo dies.

1844 Emerson publishes *Essays: Second Series*. He also delivers the address "Emancipation in the British West Indies," his first public statement against slavery.

1845 Emerson begins Representative Men lecture series.

1846 Emerson publishes *Poems*.

1847 Emerson takes his second trip to France and England.

1849 Emerson publishes *Nature*: *Addresses and Lectures*.

1850 Emerson publishes *Representative Men*.

1851 Emerson begins "The Conduct of Life" lecture series; denounces the Fugitive Slave Act of 1850 in a speech delivered in Concord, Massachusetts.

1853 Ruth Haskins Emerson dies.

1854 Henry David Thoreau publishes *Walden*.

1855 Emerson writes a letter of praise to Walt Whitman for Whitman's book *Leaves of Grass*.

1856 Emerson publishes *English Traits*.

1860 Emerson publishes *The Conduct of Life*.

1862 Thoreau dies; Emerson delivers the funeral oration.

1867 Emerson publishes *May-Day and Other Pieces*.

1868 Emerson's brother William dies.

1870 Emerson publishes *Society and Solitude*; delivers Natural History of Intellect lectures at Harvard.

1871–1873 Emerson travels to California, Europe, and Egypt.

1882 Emerson dies in Concord, Massachusetts, on April 27.

1883 Portions of the Emerson-Carlyle correspondence begin to be published.

1884 "Lectures and Biographical Sketches" published.

1893 "Natural History of the Intellect" and "Other Papers" published.

1909 "Journals," edited by sons Edward and Waldo Emerson Forbes, published in ten volumes.

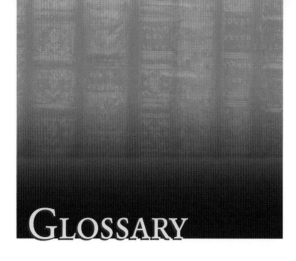

GLOSSARY

abolition The ending of slavery.

admonish To warn or express disapproval.

antiquities Ancient times, or the quality of being ancient.

articulate To express oneself clearly.

atheism The belief that God does not exist.

botany The study of plant life.

camaraderie A spirit of friendly, good fellowship.

cognition The act or process of knowing.

commodity An economic good or product.

confidante One to whom secrets are entrusted.

deliberations Discussions or debates.

denominate To name.

divinity The state of being divine or holy.

dogma Something held as an established opinion, possibly without adequate grounds.

ecstatic Referring to a state of being beyond reason and self-control.

epiphany A sudden perception of the essential nature or meaning of something.

epistemology The study of the limits of knowledge.

ethics The study of what is morally good and bad.

Gospels The first four books of the New Testament that describe the life, death, and resurrection of Jesus Christ.

integrity A firm adherence to a moral or artistic code.

intuition Quick insight.

lyceum An association providing public lectures, concerts, and entertainment

menial Unimportant.

prevailing Frequent or dominating.

prose The ordinary language people use in speaking or writing.

renounce To give up, refuse, or resign.

repatriate To go back to one's country.

rhetoric The study of speaking or writing.

skepticism The doctrine that true knowledge in a particular area is uncertain.

tangible Capable of being perceived or identified.

theologian One who studies religious faith, practice, and experience.

FOR MORE INFORMATION

The American Philosophical Foundation
31 Amstel Avenue
University of Delaware
Newark, DE 19716-4797
(302) 831-1112
Web site: www.udel.edu/apa

Concord Museum
200 Lexington Road
Concord, MA 01742
(978) 369-9763
Web site: http://www.concordmuseum.org

The Emerson Society
c/o Robert D. Habich
Department of English
Ball State University
Muncie, IN 47306
Web site: http://www.chebucto.ns.ca/Philosophy/
    Sui-Generis/Emerson/index.htm

National Underground Railroad Freedom Center
50 East Freedom Way
Cincinnati, OH 45202
(877) 648-4838
Web site: http://www.freedomcenter.org

The Society for the Advancement of American
    Philosophy (SAAP)
Dr. Kenneth Stikkers
Department of Philosophy
Southern Illinois University Carbondale
Mailcode 4505
Carbondale, IL 62901-4505
(618) 536-6641
Web site: http://www.american-philosophy.org

The Thoreau Institute at Walden Woods
44 Baker Farm
Lincoln, MA 01773
(781) 259-4700

Walden Pond State Reservation
915 Walden Street
Concord, MA 01742
(978) 369-3254

Web Sites

Due to the changing nature of Internet links, the Rosen Publishing Group, Inc., has developed an online list of Web sites related to the subject of this book. This site is updated regularly. Please use this link to access the list:

http://www.rosenlinks.com/lat/raem

For Further Reading

Allen, Gay Wilson. *Waldo Emerson; a Biography*. New York, NY: Viking Press, 1981.

Buell, Lawrence. *Literary Transcendentalism: Style and Vision in the American Renaissance*. Ithaca, NY: Cornell University Press, 1973.

Frothingham, O. B. *Transcendentalism in New England: A History*. Gloucester, MA: Smith, 1965.

King, David. *Children's Encyclopedia of American History*. London, England: DK Books, 2003.

Kramnick, Isaac. *The Portable Enlightenment Reader*. New York, NY: Penguin, 1995.

Robinson, David. *Apostle of Culture: Emerson as Preacher and Lecturer*. Philadelphia, PA: University of Pennsylvania Press, 1982.

Rohler, Lloyd. *Ralph Waldo Emerson: Preacher and Lecturer*. Westport, CT: Greenwood, 1995.

Rusk, Ralph L. *The Life of Ralph Waldo Emerson*. New York, NY: Scribners, 1949.

Simon and Parsons, eds. *Transcendentalism and its Legacy*. Ann Arbor, MI: University of Michigan Press, 1966.

Snider, Denton J. *A Biography of Ralph Waldo Emerson.* Saint Louis, MO: William Harvey Miner, 1921.

Weate, Jeremy. *Young Person's Guide to Philosophy.* London, England: DK Books, 1998.

White, David A. *Philosophy for Kids: 40 Fun Questions That Help You Wonder . . . About Everything.* Austin, TX: Prufrock Press, 2000.

BIBLIOGRAPHY

"American Unitarianism." Britannica Online. Retrieved
    August 2005 (http://search.eb.com/eb/article-40193?
    query=unitarianism&ct=).

Baker, Carlos. *Emerson Among the Eccentrics.* New York,
    NY: Viking Penguin, 1996.

"Brook Farm." Britannica Online. Retrieved August 2005
    (http://search.eb.com/eb/article-9016625).

"Enlightenment." Britannica Online. Retrieved
    August 2005 (http://search.eb.com/eb/article-
    9032680).

"Francis Bacon, Viscount Saint Alban." Britannica
    Online. Retrieved August 2005 (http://search.eb.com/
    eb/article-9108408).

"Henry David Thoreau." Britannica Online.
    Retrieved August 2005. (http://search.eb.com/eb/
    article-9072230).

"Industrial Revolution." Britannica Online. Retrieved
    August 2005 (http://search.eb.com/eb/article-
    9042370).

"Jardin des Plantes." Britannica Online. Retrieved August 2005 (http://search.eb.com/eb/article-9043381).

Kazin, Alfred, and Daniel Aaron. *Emerson: A Modern Anthology.* Boston, MA: Houghton Mifflin Company, 1958.

Kreis, Steven. *"Lectures on Modern European Intellectual History."* Historyguide.org. Retrieved January 12, 2005 (http://www.historyguide.org/intellect/lecture8a.html).

"Margaret Fuller." Britannica Online. Retrieved August 2005 (http://search.eb.com/eb/article-9035633).

More, Paul Elmer. "Emerson." *The Cambridge History of English and American Literature.* New York, NY: G. P. Putnam's Sons, 1907–1921; New York, NY: Bartleby.com, 2000. Retrieved August 2005 (http://www.bartleby.com/225/index.html#18).

"Ralph Waldo Emerson." Britannica Online. Retrieved August 2005 (http://search.eb.com/eb/article-9032526).

Richardson, Robert D., Jr. *Emerson: The Mind on Fire.* Berkeley, CA: University of California Press, 1995.

Sacks, Kenneth S. *Understanding Emerson: "The American Scholar" and His Struggle for Self-Reliance.* Princeton, NJ: Princeton University Press, 2003.

Teuber, Andreas. *Ralph Waldo Emerson.* Brandeis University. Retrieved January 22, 2005 (http://www.people.brandeis.edu/~teuber/emersonbio.html).

"Thomas Carlyle." Britannica Online. Retrieved August 2005 (http://search.eb.com/eb/article-9020374).

"Transcendentalism." Britannica Online. Retrieved August 2005 (http://search.eb.com/eb/article-9073185).

"Walt Whitman." Britannica Online. Retrieved August 2005 (http://search.eb.com/eb/article-9076878).

INDEX

ABOUT THE AUTHOR

J. Poolos is a writer and poet whose interests include philosophy and literature. He has studied the writings of Whitman, Emerson, and Thoreau. He has traveled extensively in New England and has fond memories of his visits to Concord, Massachusetts.

PHOTO CREDITS

Cover (portrait), pp. 3, 7, 20, 30, 36, 43, 71, 77, 85 Concord Free Public Library; cover (background) © Royalty-Free/Corbis; p. 11 Giraudon/Art Resource, NY; p. 12 © Science Museum, London, Great Britain/HIP/Art Resource, NY; p. 14 © Archivo Iconografico, S.A./Corbis; pp. 16, 28, 54 Private Collection/ Bridgeman Art Library; p. 19 © Massachusetts Historical Society, Boston, MA, USA/Bridgeman Art Library; pp. 22, 57, 88 © Bettmann/ Corbis; pp. 24–25, 68, 82 © Getty Images, p. 26 Massachusetts Historical Society; p. 28 (inset) © North Wind Picture Archive; p. 35 Scala/Art Resource, NY; pp. 39, 50–51 © Gianni Dagli Orti/Corbis; p. 40 © Kevin Fleming/ Corbis; pp. 44, 92 © Time-Life Pictures/Getty Images; p. 52 © Dickens House Museum, London, UK/ Bridgeman Art Library; p. 55 The Art Archive/ Culver Pictures; p. 55 (inset) © British Library, London, Great Britain/HIP/ Art Resource, NY; pp. 58, 61, 64, 90 Library of Congress Prints and Photographs Division; p. 59 The Schlesinger Library, Radcliffe Institute, Harvard University; p. 81 National Portrait Gallery, Smithsonian Institution/ Art Resource,NY; p. 94 © Sandy Felsenthal/Corbis.

Designer: Gene Mollica; **Photo Researcher:** Martin A. Levick